Dear Reader,
Here are pieces from the depths of my heart and soul. I believe life is a lot like a journey and we miss out on much of it by focusing too much on the destination. We set goals and most of the time it's not the goal that is the reward, but the wisdom we acquire along the way and the experience we gain while striving to meet them. Something important that I've learned through my time here and analyzing my own life, my struggles, my growth, my pain, is that every moment and I mean every moment is a chance to learn something even if it's learning what not to do again or perhaps be a little kinder to ourselves for our past mistakes. Happiness, love, wealth or anything that is our goal, we must learn that unless we are truly content within our hearts that we'll never be satisfied with the outcome of whatever the universe may have gifted us with. To put things in the simplest of terms, in this little book you'll find snapshots of my journey in the form of poetry.

Yours Truly,

Jacob

I don't know where I'm going, but I do know that if I walk gently and love fiercely then I just have to end up somewhere beautiful. Will you walk with me?

All of our lives we are told, what to believe, what to think, what success looks like, who to love, and we call ourselves free.

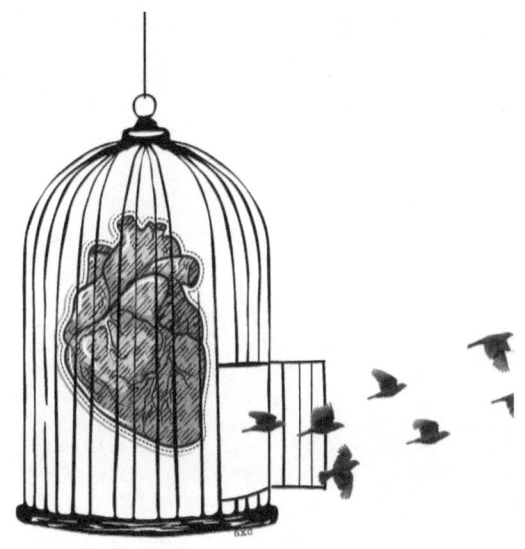

I'll smile for today. I won't cry over yesterday's mistakes and I won't fret over the uncertainty of tomorrow. I'll smile because I've made it this far. Will you smile with me?

You shouldn't share your body with anyone that doesn't appreciate your mind. You shouldn't share your mind with anyone that doesn't appreciate your heart. You shouldn't share your heart with anyone that doesn't appreciate your soul. You're more than just a good time. You're worth more than gold.

You're not weird, you're real. You're not strange because you feel. It's not that people don't like you. It frightens them because you have the courage to take on every emotion and the way you turn it into something so different, so beautiful, it's brave, it's raw, it's a strange to them. That's a terribly frightening in a world gone numb.

Don't try to figure me out, you'll only drive yourself crazy. Don't try to label me, you'll only push me away. I'm not like other people, at least not many. I used to be asleep, I used to be numb, I used to be blind, I used to be dumb. I wish I could snap my fingers and go back to that because I never asked for this and I'd gladly give it back. I know that's impossible though, so I'll keep pushing on. I'll keep ripping myself apart and bleeding these words, hoping maybe you might see me. Hoping maybe, just maybe, you might feel something too, and you might see that I'm as real as you.

We drive the same cars,
wear the same clothes,
live in the same houses,
just the same old cookie-cutter
life out of that drab old box and they
wonder what's missing.

More often than not
it's ourselves.

What do you do for fun? Well, every once in a while I take my pain and turn it into art. I take my love and share it with the world. I take all of me and put it out there for you to hopefully feel something too. That's what I do. How about you?

My own truths. I sometimes wrestle with my ego and when I meet someone new I always think about the aftermath. Did they get the real me or that mask of macho, angst, or insecurity.

Most things in life I've learned through experience. Here are a few of mine.

Look that woman in her eyes, don't stare down at her body.

Listen to that man's message before you laugh at his voice.

Speak to people from your heart, don't blabber from the head.

Things can't always be taught by hearing and seeing.

The hardest lessons in life are learned by doing and feeling.

The mind can play tricks on you sometimes, but make no mistake. The heart won't ever lie to you or lead you astray. The head can be a dreamscape or it can be a nightmare, but the heart is where dreams meet reality. Let go of self judgement and the fear of falling. Learn to lean in and embrace your calling.

What if instead of teaching girls to look pretty in makeup, we taught them to appreciate their own skin, body, and essence of who they really are. What if instead of teaching boys to man up, we taught them to embrace their emotions and express them in healthy ways. What if we actually let our children be themselves and didn't tell them who they should emulate. How different would the world look?

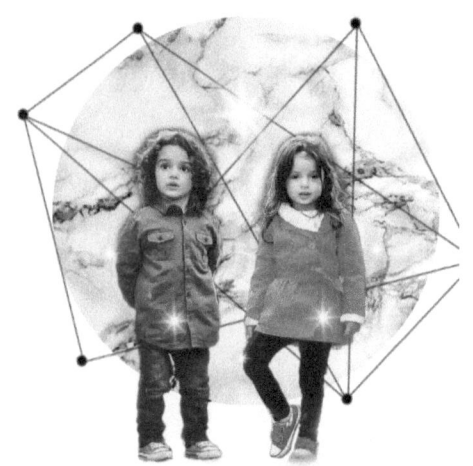

That's the thing about "self-love" they don't tell you. It's not always easy or pretty, it's downright hard sometimes. Some days it doesn't feel like love at all because there are days when you will have trouble even liking yourself and appreciating life, but... there's always a but, it's love because you haven't given up. No matter how many times you've failed at whatever life has thrown at you and sometimes you've even gotten the best of yourself. You're still here and you're worthy. That's love, never giving up.

How'd you survive?

The light in my heart was brighter than the darkness that clouded my mind.

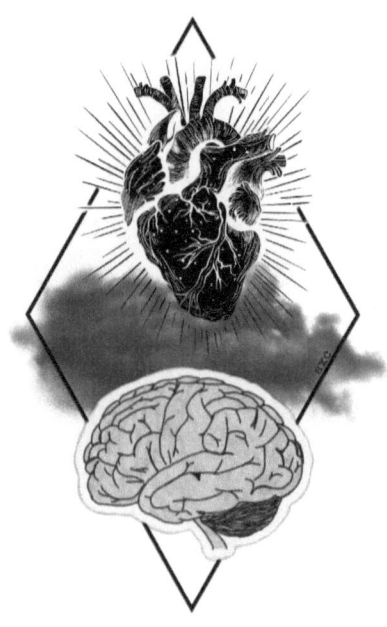

You can't fix people. You can't and you
shouldn't try to, but you can love them.
That's all they really need anyway.
That's what we all need and sometimes by
loving another we fix what is broken
inside of us.

I'd lost myself in that world and then I found myself in poetry. I'm making my way back, but it's going to be a new one this time. I'm bringing magic with me.

You better start loving yourself or no one else will. Not the flawless one that you pretend to be online either. The one there in the mirror with all of your flaws, scars, the mistakes that weigh heavily on your soul, but you still manage to smile because you know that more than anything you're still worth way more than you can imagine. Smile, feel it, believe it because it's true.

"It Loves"

You think that you can control it,
who gets in.
You can try,
you can run,
you can deny,
but the mind thinks,
the lungs breathe,
and the heart it just beats,
and yearns,
and loves.

It loves.

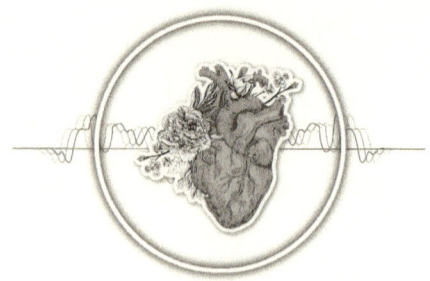

I want to kiss all night and dance until we're sweaty, have a few too many drinks and Uber home. We'll throw our clothes off in the kitchen and make our way to the bath. Put on some Otis and light a few candles. You can sit in front of me and lean back while I wrap my arms around you. I'll massage your head and kiss your neck while you sing and tell me stories. When we've finally made it out of the bath, we'll dance our way to the bed. I want to hold you all night and feel your warmth next to me and maybe when we awake in the morning, the ice that surrounds our hearts will have melted.

Ask yourself, are they adding sunshine to your skies or are they making them hazy and gray? I know I'm not afraid of the the rain. Give me sunshine or give me the rain... but by no means do I want to stay stuck in the fog.

About me... Part of me is sunrises, poetry, flowers, and birds singing sweet melodies. The other, well that's cold steel and an ocean of cascading flames that I just can't apologize for.

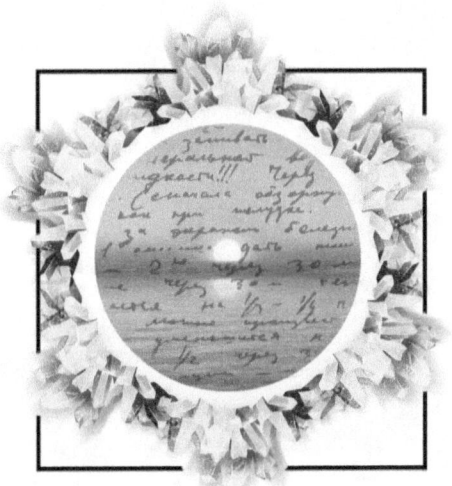

I like when people tell stories about themselves and their experiences. It opens up little doors and shows you what it's like inside of the their world. It takes you outside of yourself, gives you better perspective when you return to your own thoughts. It's how we connect and reflect, that's really special when I think about it.

It saddens me to meet people that aren't passionate about anything. People that've been wearing a mask for so long that they don't even realize they have it on anymore. They're breathing, but they aren't alive. I want to shake them, scream, anything to get a rise out of them, but I don't. I'm afraid my mask will fall off too.

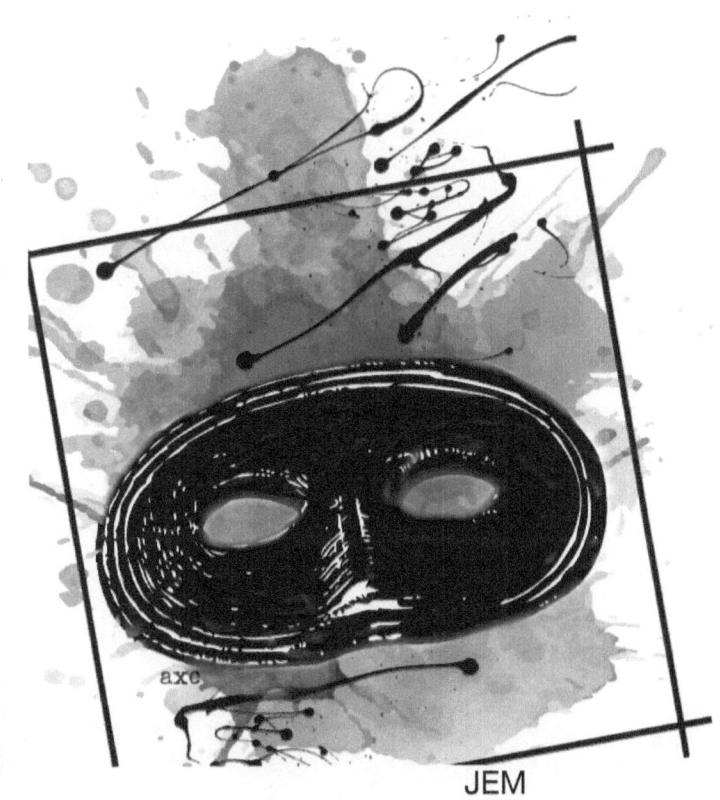

I'd caught it, seems like most poets have at least once in their life. I was numb, afraid of happiness, it never lasted. The sadness becomes so normal that it doesn't even get you by surprise anymore. I'd have to cut myself open just feel that I was alive. I was tired of living that way. I'd hoped and dreamed for something better. Then one day when I slit myself open, there was letter in front of letter, word upon word of things I'd never spoke, things I'd thought I'd never do. Good feelings and sunshine blooming inside of me, all because of you, poetry. You saved me.

I don't see success as a fancy title, plaque on the wall, or the numbers in someone's bank account. While those are grand attributes to climb the economic ladder in life. I view success by how someone treats people and the feeling that they leave them with. The peace that they've been able to find within their hearts amidst this chaotic world. Those are the ones that I envy, the ones I aspire to be like. One day I hope to succeed.

I ate pizza in the bath tub and drank red wine. Soulful tunes echoed out of the speaker on the counter. The water steamed as I relaxed, a bead of sweat ran down my forehead and my cheek, right down to my lips and I licked them. It was salty and I laughed at myself after for how silly I must look to a fly on the wall. Mmm, but the taste still reminded me of you, and in between laughing, I paused and zoned out for a second. I remembered you, your salty skin by the beach that night, no one else there except for us and the full moon. The waves crashing, but gently, the breeze kissed our skin and I kissed your neck. I didn't know what love was, but this was maybe close in my book. And now looking back, I know that it was.

You have to get lost, really lost, fucking lose all of what you've been taught, all of what they'd told you was anything to realize that you are everything you'll ever need.

I fell in love with the colors of the sunset today and in a matter of seconds they were gone. Kind of reminded me of you, guess it's about time that I should just move on.

Your heart broke open because the world needs the love that's inside of you.

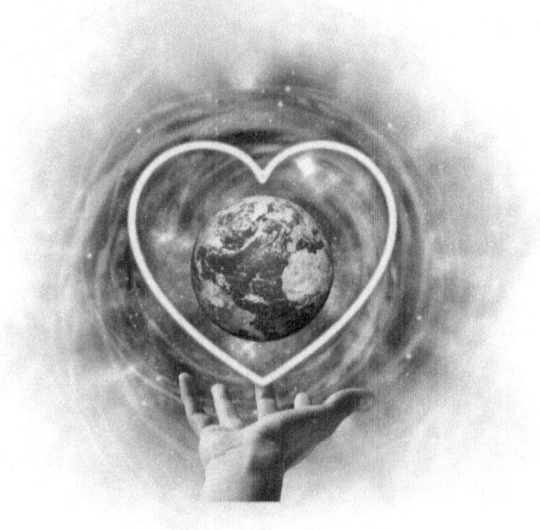

I'm trying to be that person
I was before my heart
ever got broken.
Will you try
with me?

Love, my dear is not something
that you should have to compete
for. It is what you're made of and
you are deserving of just as much.

No dear...

Never compete, you are deserving
and even if you don't believe it yet.
It's ok. I'll show you.

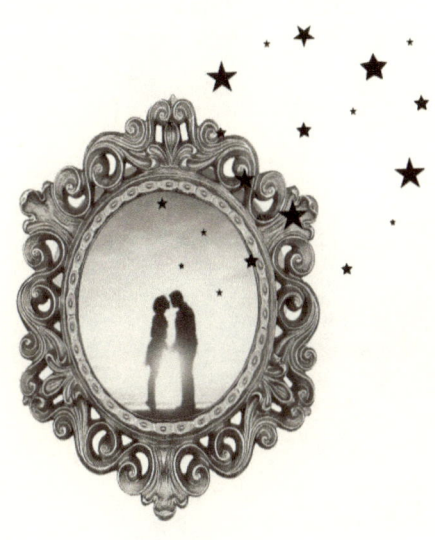

Take me down to your river where rays of sunshine glisten.

Where the water rushes over the rocks.

It's like music if we listen.

Take me there without expectations or obligations.

Take me there and I hope that maybe, just maybe there will be enough momentum to float me down into your ocean.

I would rather be understood
than loved, for if you were to
understand me then I would
truly feel loved.

If you'd say I get you, rather
than I love you, then darling
you'd get me.

All of me.

Until you learn to love everything that is
you, then you'll waste the time of
everyone that universe sends your way.
Until you learn to love the broken pieces,
the flaws, and the mistakes. You'll never
be ready to give because you'll think that
nobody has what it takes.

I wonder if I ever cross your mind when you're putting your hair up in front of the mirror while your bath is running. I'm right there behind you with my head there resting on your shoulder, my hands tracing the outlines of your silhouette, stopping and squeezing on your softest parts. I'm kissing your neck gently and nibbling on your ear lobe. Do you feel me pressing up against you?

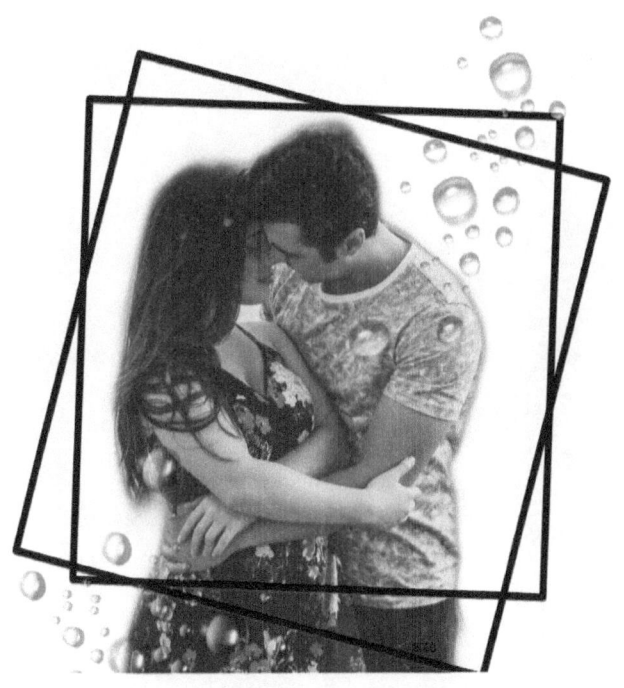

You should be the one that they dream of even when their eyes are wide open, it's 3pm, and they're stone cold sober on Monday afternoon.

The world is crazy? No, sweetheart. The world is a beautiful miracle and so are you because there's a whole universe inside of you. Don't let the simple minds get you down with their negativity. I know there's more to you than what you see. There is a volcano in your heart and stars in your bones. There's more power inside of you than you can comprehend. Your soul is timeless, infinite, everlasting... There is no end.

That pain you're feeling was meant for you, maybe not that person, but that pain you're feeling it was meant for you to know. It's how the mold is broken. It is how you grow.

We danced in the kitchen, an old cover by
The Bee Gees played. I spun you around
and hugged you from behind. We swayed
there for a second, my chin in the crease
of your neck. It smelled like heaven with
a dash of heartbreak. I inhaled you and
kissed up to your earlobes and you turned
and looked at me. One of those looks
where our eyes spoke. We kept on, and
then danced some more. And I don't think
that you know what it's like.

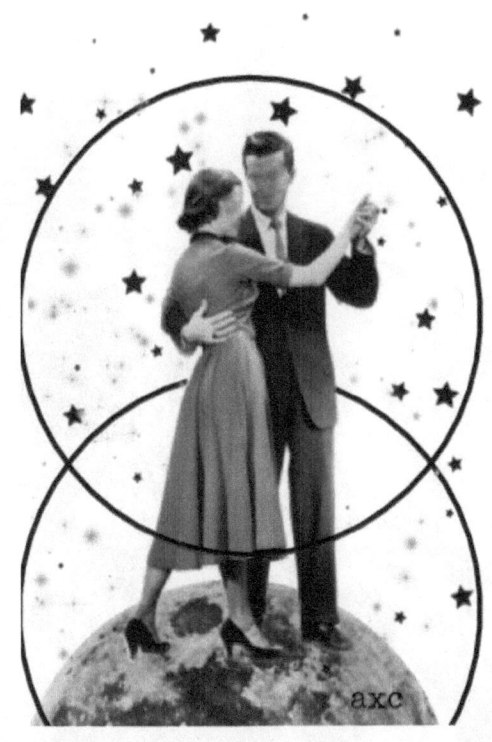

In this life many may touch you, but there will be few that will hold your body, keep your heart safe, and love you all the way down to your soul; the way that you're supposed to be loved. These are the ones you hold on to.

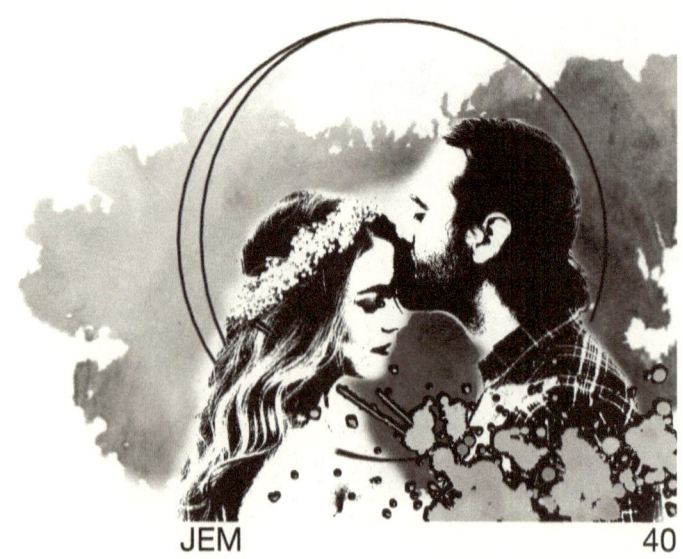

You didn't only hold my hand. You held my heart. You didn't only kiss my lips. You kissed my soul. I didn't just give you my time. I showed you the deepest corners of my mind, but that wasn't enough and it never would've been. You still craved more stuff.

There is no finding yourself. There's only uncovering someone who was there all along and learning how to let that person be.

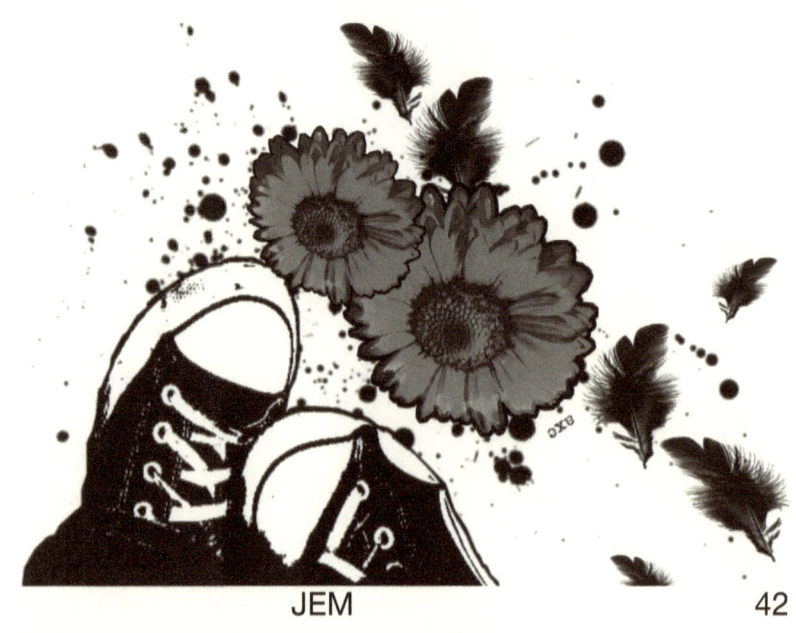

Some days I feel free.

Sometimes I feel that
I keep replaying and
reliving every mistake
that I've ever made.

I feel bound to everyone
that's been successful at
making me their fool.

Wrapped up in chains of doubt
and stuck behind a wall with
no getting out.

It's like I'll never find the key.

Some days I feel free.

Someday I will be.

Whether we want to admit it or not, we all have it. That ego that gets a little trampled once in a while, just enough to knock us off balance and we feel we have to react. We do things or say things out of anger and sometimes hurt those closest to us, by then it's too late. Once the stone is thrown, there is no taking it back, but we can own up to it. We can acknowledge the damage we've caused and we can say two words that if said right and meant can help mend a broken heart or ease a worried mind... I'm sorry.

And look at you with a raging river of love flowing through your veins, soon you'll be home. I know you feel lost sometimes, but it won't be long before you've run into the ocean.

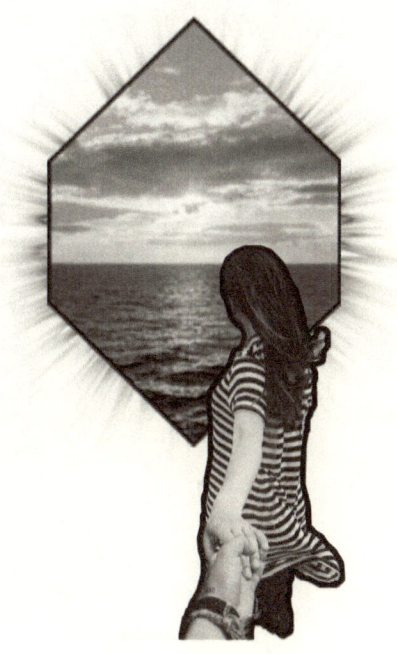

Tell me about sunrises, birds singing sweet tunes, and spring flowers blooming. Tell me about full moons, thunderstorms, and sizzling summer nights. Tell me about autumn colors, leaves falling, and blowing away in the crisp air. Tell me about the first snow in the winter, warm cider, and snuggling up by the fire. Tell me stories of all the seasons and how they make you feel. Tell me what you believe in and everything that is real. Tell me what you love the most and why. Tell me about life and where you think that we go when we die. Tell me your dreams and wishes. Tell me all about your fear. Tell me anything and everything, I'll sit right here. Right here by your side and listen to every word. I'll listen to it all because it matters to me and so do you. Tell me that you want me, just like I want you.

I loved you a little more even after you left. I found that it hurt less than to hate and I felt it even if it was a little too late.

The waves were crashing over me. That darkness taking over me. Those demons took control of me. No one grabbing hold of me. They just stand there and watch me drown. Sinking deeper and deeper down.
On the outside I may have looked fine, but inside I was losing my mind. I lost sight of the shore. Distorted view of the light. It was only me that could win that fight. I'll have to swim on my own. I'll make it back this time alone.

Put your hand on my chest.
Do you feel how strong that is?

"Yes"

That's because of you.
You didn't give up on me.
That's why I'm here and
I'll never give up
on you.

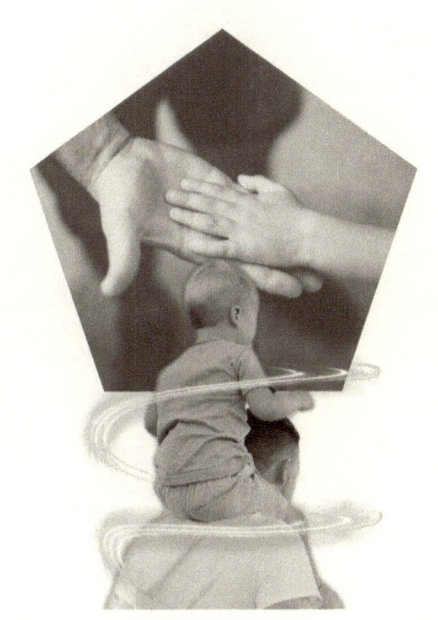

The sun painted a masterpiece over the horizon this morning. The birds were all singing and dancing as the wind hummed a melody through tall oak trees. The whole world was alive and awake in this moment, except for my heart. My heart was still wrapped in that bed with the girl who wasn't there.

I wonder if it's me that you see when those pretty eyes of yours close because I see you everywhere even when mine are open. I wonder if it's me that see because that's what I was hoping.

Some are made for the beach and the ocean's salty air. Some love the forest, the mountains, nature and the countryside. Some favor the city, bright lights and buildings scraping the sky. I don't care for any of it in particular, I really don't care. It's all quite drab to me unless you are there.

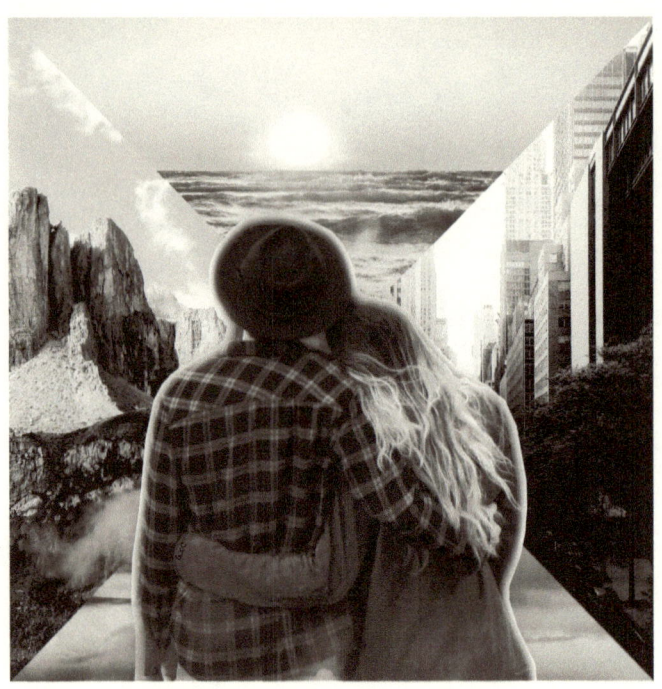

There's a dreamer in my heart and realist in my head. They argue sometimes, the realist usually convinces the dreamer that he's right and he backs down, but there's magician that lives in my soul and sometimes shows up and tricks them both.

If not madly,
then how?
I don't know,
nor do I care to.

Freedom feels a lot like loneliness
when you don't have anyone
to share it with.

I want to smile because I'm happy, because I feel it, even if just for the moment, not just because someone is taking my picture.

On those days that you
don't feel so shiny just
remember babe; that
even the sun goes down.

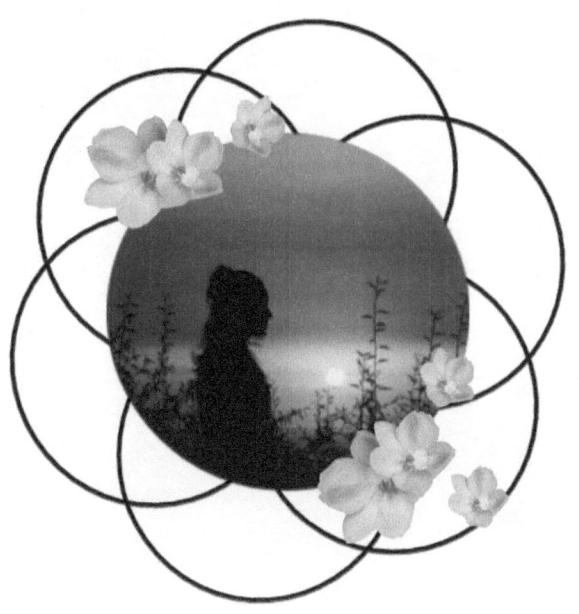

Say what's really on your mind not just what you think people want to hear. This is how you find out where you belong and where you belong isn't always where you've fit in.

Every time that you judge,
you miss a chance to love.
Every time you're jealous,
you miss a chance to connect.
Before you throw that stone,
take some time, reflect.

We overthink too much,
when the truth is that
we don't love anyone
from our minds.

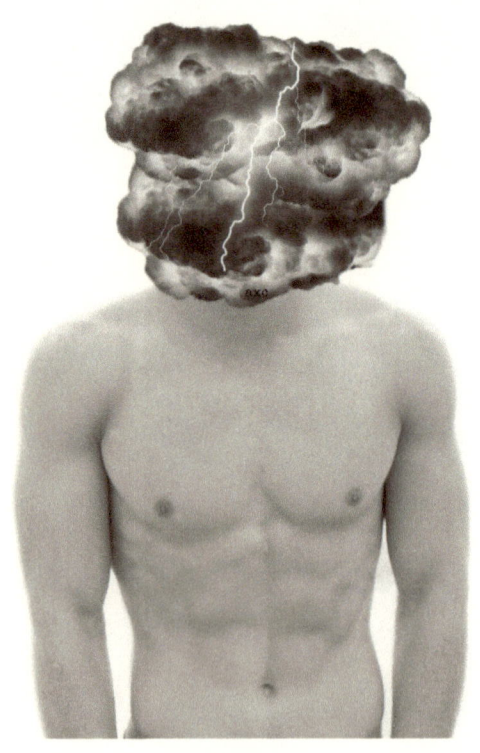

I'm sorry if I didn't
love you right when I
hadn't yet learned to
love myself.

You'll search and search, but you won't dare recognize them by sight. You'll have to learn a new language if you truly want to find what's real. If you allow yourself to be open, honest and vulnerable, then and only then will you know, not by what you see or think, but by the way they make you feel.

What do I want to be remembered as?
Nothing too extravagant, maybe just a
friend that made you laugh at the bullshit
imposed on all of us and said to be happy
being the beautiful, flawed, imperfect you
that everyone else is scared to.

Silly child that's why you feel so lost.
You're looking with your eyes when you
should be searching with your soul and
feeling with your heart.

Not everyone can handle someone like that. Someone that loves like there's no tomorrow.

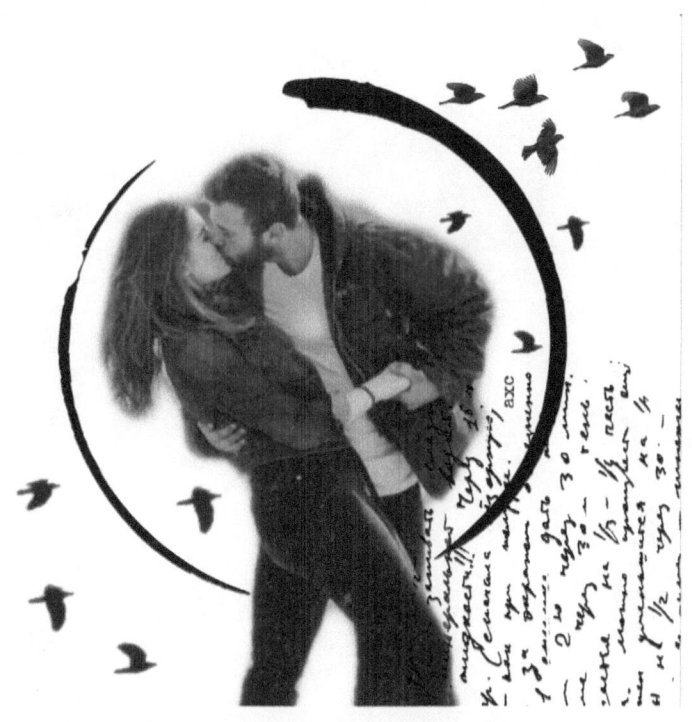

Twenty six letters, over one hundred seventy thousand words and the only one I can think of is you.

I can feel the hell inside of your chest and wonder why I feel like I'm in heaven sitting next to you. Maybe it's because mine is beating the same hellacious tune. Maybe I'm comfortable next to chaos.

And I'll keep on
chasing them,
the stars,
full moons,
sunsets,
happiness,
and her.

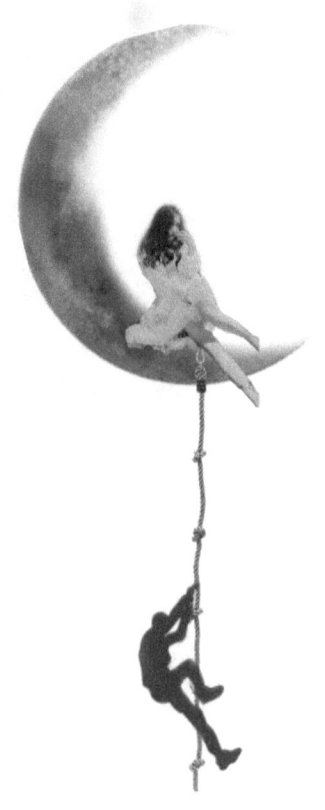

Meet me in the space
between black and white.
The space where magic hides.
Meet me in the gray.

I will make you feel something because that's what I do. Whether it's love or hate, you'll feel something. I promise you that because I won't allow you to be so fucking numb anymore. I'm going to give you the truth and you'll either love me or hate me for it.

Maybe that's why they
put them way up there
in the sky, so that when
it's dark all around we'd
have a reason to keep
looking up.

It was really dark inside
here tonight, but then
you walked in with that
fire in your eyes and
suddenly I felt like
looking up.

I remember that night,
you were by my side,
hand in hand and
you stared at
the moon.

I was looking at
you.

It's exhausting to have a mind that thinks so much and a heart that just wants to feel. Both of them can get overspent and making it hard to tell what is real.

You tell me that I should quit.
That it's killing me, but I'm already walking around feeling like a ghost.
I don't even know if I'm breathing until I take a pull on it and the watch as the smokes drifts away as I exhale and then I disappear.

You took most of it when you left, but I still have enough to make beautiful poetry with. Someday you'll read them and wonder; how does one make such beautiful words out of something so broken?

"Emotional Paradox"

Often it's quite peculiar
these paradoxical
feelings of mine.

I welcome pain with a
smile because I've
found it to be the most
trustworthy.

While happiness I've
begun to mistrust because
it's always looking
for the exit door.

So this is how I ended.

She pulled frayed heart strings from my ears and balled them up in knots until she had enough rope to tie me up.

She pressed her lips on mine, sweet and salty like caramel with hints of ocean was the taste I got as she sucked my soul out in front of me and chewed on it.

She elegantly walked away as I lied there breathless, motionless, skin drought of all moisture and color.

I heard a violin playing in the distance and saw a pale blue light.

Is this the end, is this how it really feels to die?

Nobody around to witness what has taken place.

You make me laugh
and to me that's
kind of like
love.

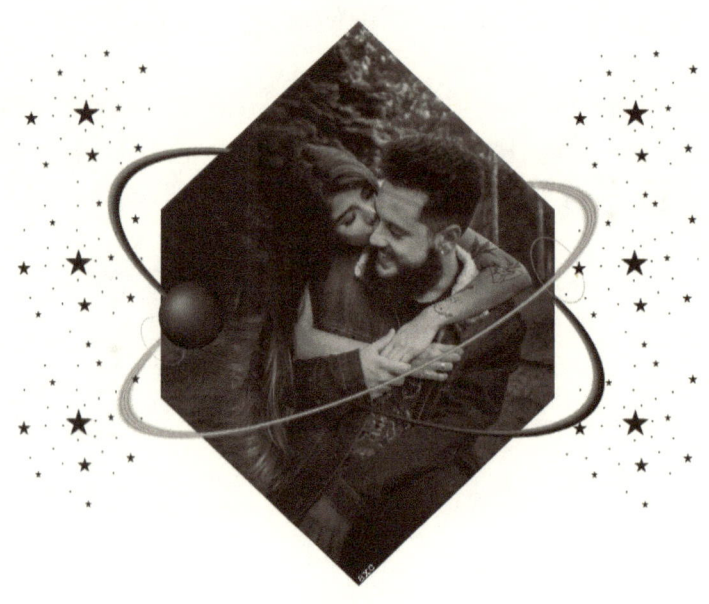

I looked at her and it
broke my heart to see
my lies dripping down
her cheeks.

Darling, don't you understand?
Not being loved back isn't
such a terrible thing.
Not being able to love is
much, much worse.

Don't confuse love with admiration. One is only there for you when you're doing well; the other stays by your side even if you walk through hell.

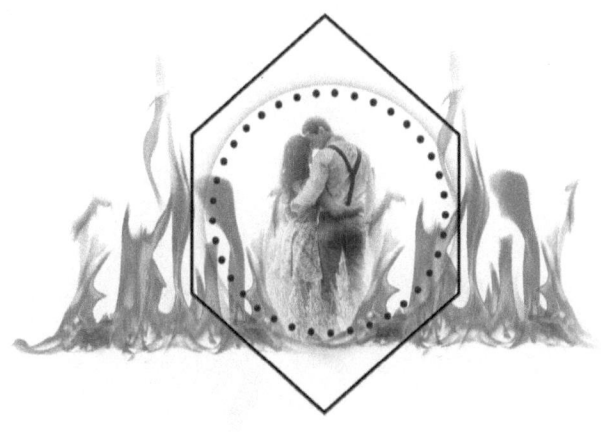

I fell in love with the stars sometime ago way up there in the sky and when we first met you had them too right there in your eyes.

The light kissed you on your cheek and
glistened off your eyes. Your lips
sparkled as my name slid off your tongue
and I don't know what you call that
feeling you gave me.

For the right one you won't ever be too much. The right one will love your flaws and comfort your insecurities. The right one will see your light and your dark. They'll love you for all of your being. You just wait, I'll show you.

The way that you smiled at me made me believe for a little while that it wasn't just you and I. It made me believe there was an us.

Compassion - When we listen with empty ears and a full heart. It's where we send egos to die. Love lives there and thrives.

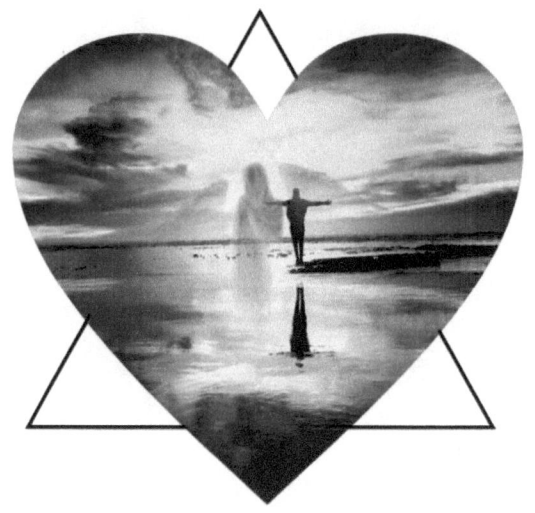

When I close my eyes
and listen to my heart,
between the thumps,
there is a whisper,
gently calling out,
saying only your name.
Tell me darling.
Does yours ever
do the same?

If you're going to hold on, which I know
is always our first instinct, then by all
means darling... hold on to yourself.

And never, ever, let go
again.

I hope that someday, someone will make you believe that you're worth loving and that you'll be brave enough to let them.

I hope that person is you.

I believe it's about contentment. If we aren't content with ourselves, then we'll never be content with another no matter how great they are, or what they have to offer is. The happiness will be short lived like buying a new pair of shoes or a fancy new car. All of these things are external pacifiers for the ego, when our search for joy should start from within. Find out what moves your soul and makes your heart full. Spend your life doing more of that.

People don't like real, they don't like raw. They like things that are sold, things that are bought. Price tags, numbers, and labels. They've confused happy with egocentricity. I just want the simple things. Sunrises and coffee. Full moons and gin. Good music and food, maybe a couple good friends.

There's daylight, moonlight, starlight,
Firelight, and electricity.
Then there is
She.

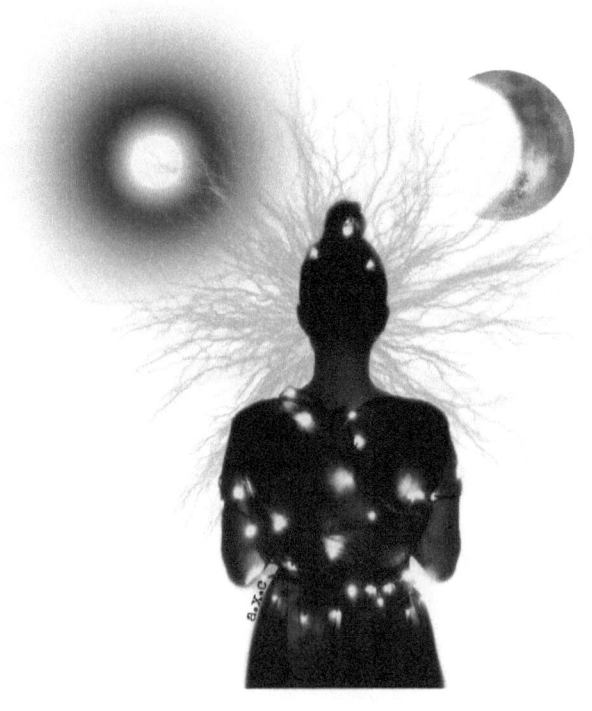

It's been so long that I barely remember your face. I used to know the feel of it even with my eyes closed. And all those memories, I barely think of them at all anymore. But every once in a while when the Sun is setting and it's quiet for a second. Yes, even the birds stop chirping. I hear the universe whisper your name. And I think to myself, do you ever hear the same?

Her arms around me feels like home, her legs around me an adventure. She's the best of both worlds.

"Lovers Guilt"

I'm guilty,
guilty of loving
when I should've left.

I'm guilty,
guilty of leaving
when I should've loved.

I'm guilty,
guilty in all aspects.
I'll bear the cross,
I'll wear the blame.

I'm guilty,
guilty of kissing
another while I
was thinking nothing
but your name.

Perhaps my only legacy will be the love that I leave behind. So, I'll love like there's no tomorrow because who knows, maybe there isn't a next time.

I often overdo things. It's just the way I am. I'm overly loving, overly sensitive, overly stubborn; my soul is pure, but for the time being I'm just a man.

You were decorated with warning labels and I drank you to the last drop. I smoked you till the last ash and I didn't want to stop. Now I'm shaking and I'm twitching, craving just another taste. Stuck to wallow in this madness, missing your touch, your lips, your face.

Stars in her eyes, lips sweet as honey.
That girl is the moon on two legs.

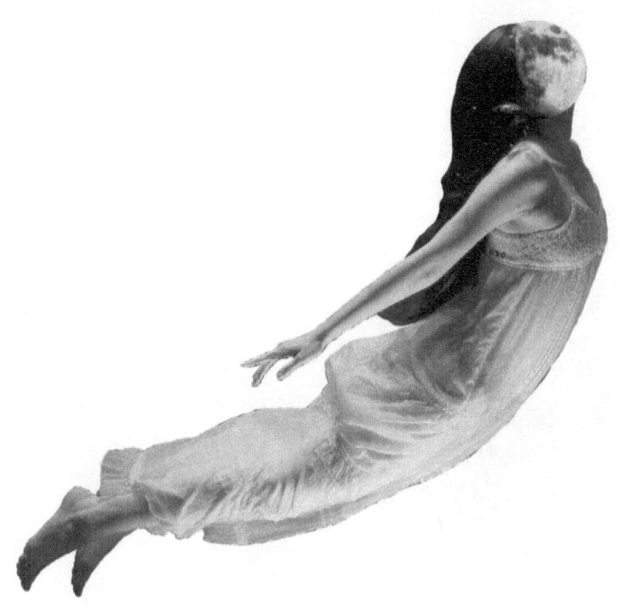

She has a Universe in her eyes, oceans in her touch, cascading flames in her soul. Her touch would rebirth me into another existence because until her, a kiss wasn't a kiss. Not from any other, not like this.

We had a thing between us, a connection, a sort of sexual alchemy if you will. We needn't say much at all, our bodies were doing all the talking.

Somehow our bodies gravitated towards each other, souls intertwined, and time stopped briefly for a moment and we disrupted the entire galaxy.

"Love Artist"

Your eyes drew me in

Hands tracing outlines of my body, making me appear where before I was invisible

Lips filling in the blank spaces of what was an empty silhouette

Body painting the whole scene onto me and spilling out a work of art

You've brought me to life

Let's get in my car at midnight and drive towards tomorrow. We don't need a map or even a destination. We can get lost for a day or we can make it a vacation. We'll go somewhere that nobody knows our name. I've been itching to get away. This town is much too plain. I'll call you sweetheart and you call me baby. Let's go crazy for a little while. Does that sound too insane?

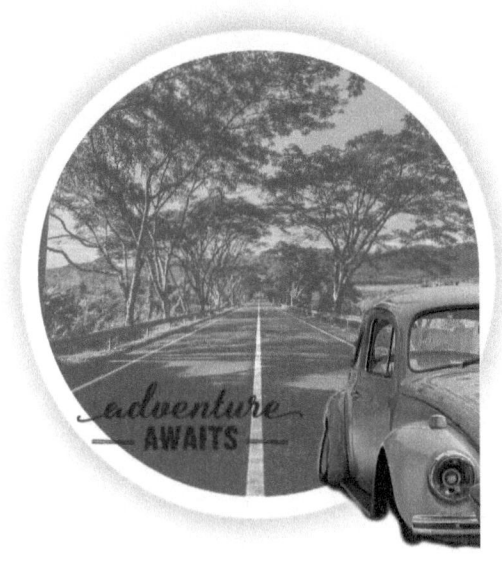

More than the raw heat and passionate desire, it's those little sweet moments when the whole universe is silent, your bodies are tangled up and your souls melt into each other's.

I've caught glimpses of it, little specks of magic that shine within moments. You can see them sparkle in the eyes of those there with you. You can't say anything though, you don't want to miss it. Everything slows down a bit; time, your breath, your thoughts and you just feel grateful for all that is around because for just a little while you're free.

You are nothing to me,
nothing at all.
If I'm hurt and dying,
I wouldn't waste my call.
You wouldn't answer,
you wouldn't care.
When I'm in need,
you're never there.
You're nothing to me,
that's what I say,
to get me through,
another day.
Because I ain't shit to you,
you've made it clear.
So, why do I still want you here?
You are nothing,
but that's a lie.
I'm all alone,
these tears I cry.

Woven into the fabric of space and time, there's a place where the threads of you and I are stitched together. It's beautiful, it really is, but if you look a little further you'll see where we unravel.

We're starving for something that we've never tasted. An undying thirst that just can't be quenched. We're languishing here wrapped up in pale silence, when we should be covered in vibrant hues of love and laughter. How will we ever find what we seek? Maybe we can, if we look in the mirror again, just take a peek. It's right there it starts with you. If you want the truth, then just be true.

I hope that you find it, whatever it is
that you're missing. I hope that you
realize that it does not stem from others.
The wicked words off of your tongue meant
to harm another. That could never make
one happy. How could you act so content
by making others feel inadequate.

Falling isn't something that interest me.
Just the sound of it is so detrimental to
your health, like you'd be useless after,
done. Nope, not for me, not anymore. I'd
prefer to grow like a seed placed down in
the warm soil and every day you give it a
little more water, a little more light,
and a lot more love. Roots digging down
deeper, so deep it'd take an act of God to
ever knock it down. So falling, no baby I
don't think I can, but growing with you.
I feel that with all that I am.

On the outside she's not that different at all, but oh, on the inside... She's butterflies, dragons and wild waterfalls.

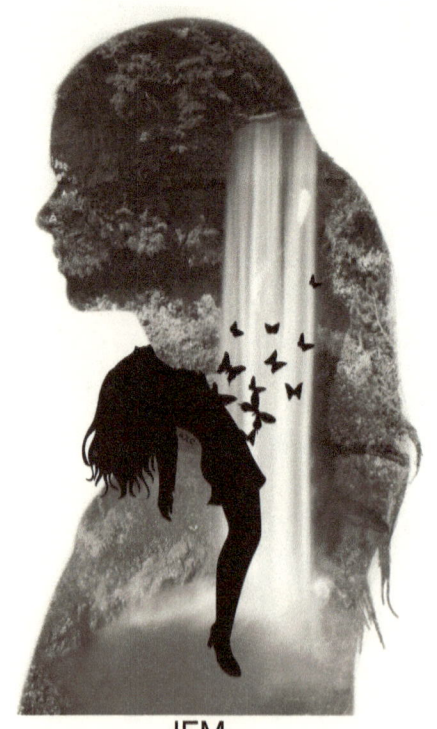

JEM

We're all beautiful and fragile

I've seen the toughest breakdown

And I've seen the smallest rise up

Whether we want to or not

We must keep on

Keep rising

Keep falling

Keep searching

Keep finding

Keep giving

Keep loving

Keep trying

After you finally find it,
your fire, then you won't
waste any time around those
who don't feed your flames.

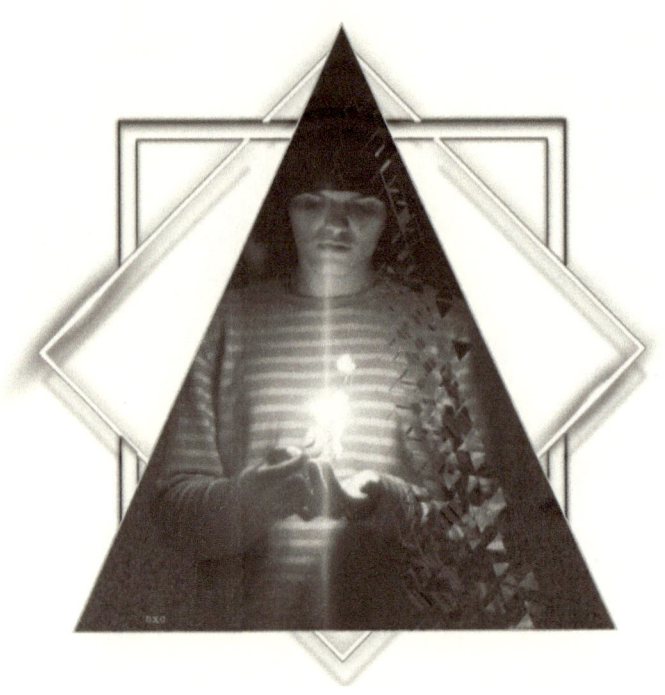

Some are thinkers and others feelers, but the poet is both. What a curse of a gift that can be at times, turning broken hearts into prose and rhymes.

Can we differentiate between what is thought and what is felt? We try time and time again to make sense of something that seems damn impossible to articulate and it's as if we're all stuck romanticizing about something that we may have never had anyway. If we did have it then tell me why we threw it away. Why'd we seek more if what we had was real? Perhaps we couldn't tell the difference between what we said and what we feel.

On a summer's night we lied down on the warm concrete after the sun had gone down and the stars were shining bright. I'd point to this one and you that one, we'd name them. I remember you called yours Felix and I called mine Carmen. For a split second which felt like minutes, we'd be projected out into the galaxy, so close that we could almost shake hands with them. Then in the blink of an eye we'd be right back down on the warm driveway, sweating, laughing, as you said "Dad, I love you, now let's go inside. The mosquitoes are biting me."

Before we can become who we're meant to be, we have to take a good look at our own mistakes, the negative behaviors, the patterns that for one reason or another keep showing up in our lives. We can't place blame on others and we shouldn't keep condemning ourselves to hell for the sins of our youth or our past. We have to look forward, move forward, and keep moving in the right direction regardless of what we've been through or done, the only way to be a failure is to choose to stay down in that negative mindset. I've made decisions out of impulse, out of desire, out of spite. I've wanted to give up on myself at times and there were times that I didn't even want to live, but for some reason I held on, I held on even on the darkest days because I knew that there was a light inside stronger than the darkness that I'd surrounded myself with, a light begging to get out, a light that was meant to shine and it will shine through me.

I believe more than any other longing in our lifetime, we long to return to the purest form of light that exists. The light that created us and is and forever will be calling us until we return home.

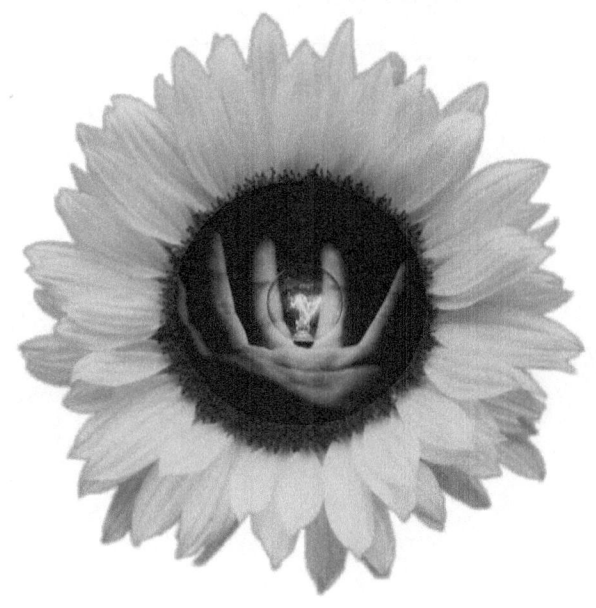

One day, between all of the things said and not meant and the things meant and never said there will always be little pieces of us that we left behind. Little pieces of our hearts that we'll never get back, that we'll never give another because those little pieces will always belong to each other, but you see even those little pieces, though sometimes we think that we may have lost, we realize later that they are worth the price, because sometimes love, it cost losing. Just make sure they're worth it.

Sweetie, It's knocking
on your door.
How long are you
going to leave it out there.

That soul of yours,
I know you can hear it.
It's loud and clear.

It's waiting for you,
on the other side
of fear.

Poetry is the bleeding truth for all of us carnivorous liars.

It's for the frayed heart strings and the souls on fire.

The insomniac hopeless romantics with regret in the backs of their throats.

The indigo children connected to the earth and the stars.

The ones inhibited by social norms with a pen in hand.

For all of the ones feeling heartache over things they've forgotten to say.

It is living, breathing, alive and well, poetry is here to stay.

I'd never made love before just by sitting in the same room as someone, but that's what we were doing before our lips ever spoke a word.

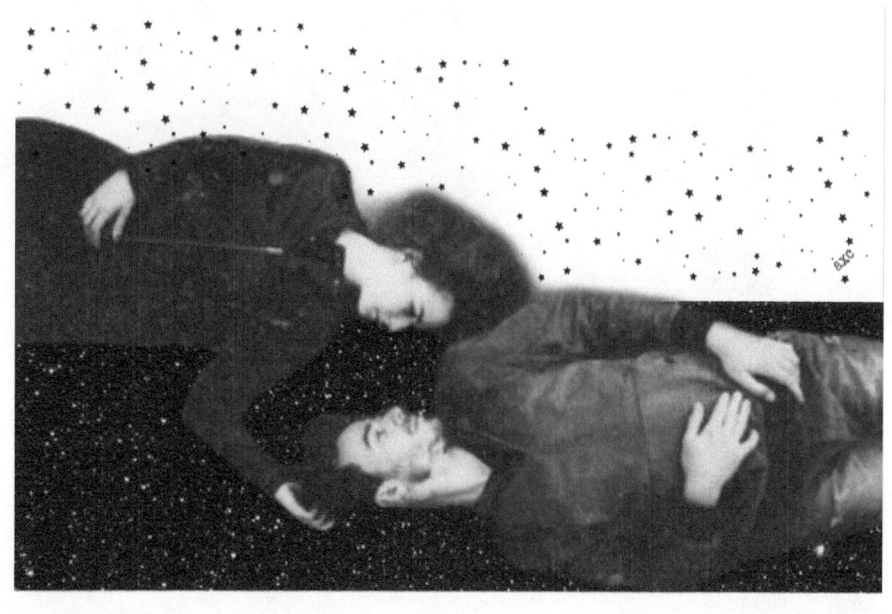

Since seeing it,
I hope that there's
never a day that
you go without it.
That smile of yours,
it's magic.

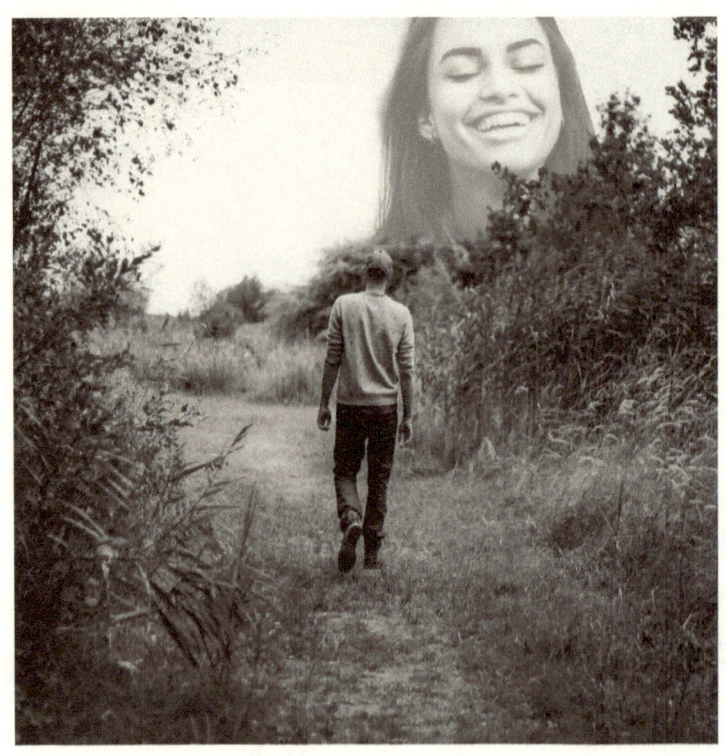

It's not something for the
weak. It's not easy and it's
not to played with. It's for
those not afraid to bleed,
those willing to put up a fight.
It's right here and so are we.
Will you be brave with me
tonight?

"Cold Flame"

The night is young,
the moon is new.

The fire is crackling,
your eyes are blue.

I watch it burn,
I feel the flames.

I see us dancing,
I hear your name.

Red wine sipped slow,
smoke in the air.

I can feel you on me,
but no ones there.

It comes in waves

All of it

Love, Laughter, Sadness, Realization

It comes so fiercely crashing from every direction imaginable then it retracts back to calm solace smooth as glass

Adjust your sails accordingly

Move with it, flow with it, ride it out

And never believe that the waters will remain rough eternally

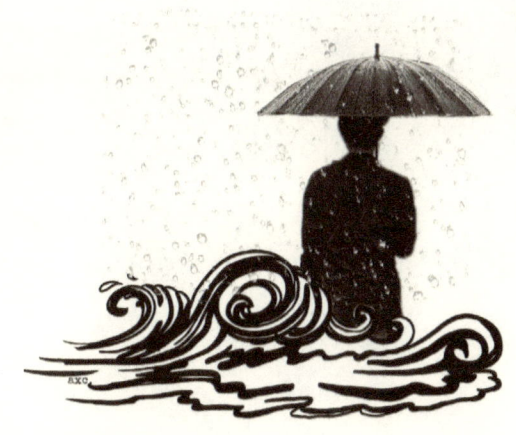

That's how it is sometimes. Sometimes, you're just the crazy one in the room when you're an adult who still possesses imagination. Everyone one else is filling up on the numbness that society dishes out and you are just a little crazy because you believe in magic.

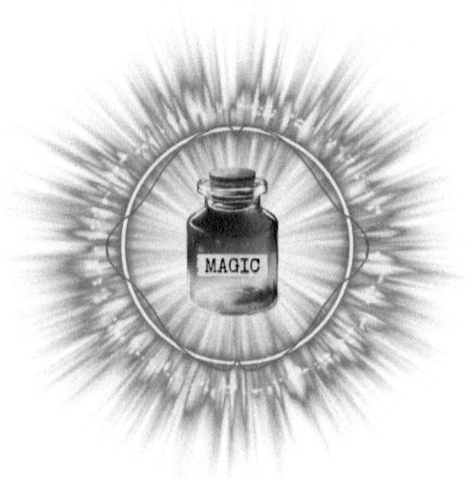

Everyone has their demons.
That's what they tell me.
If you believe that then
you must believe that
we have our angels too.
I've seen them with
my own eyes.

Believe it, both are true.

But to me it is love,
it's vulnerable, naked,
deep, raw passion and you
most definitely shouldn't
share it with someone
whom you don't.

Darling did you ever think that the way you long to be loved isn't love at all. It's just an exaggeration of the ego. Real love would never cage you when you're meant to be free. Real love would never ask you to be anything, but just to be.

The days that we let love win are always a little easier to remember. If it's love that you're fighting for then just let go, drop your guard, surrender.

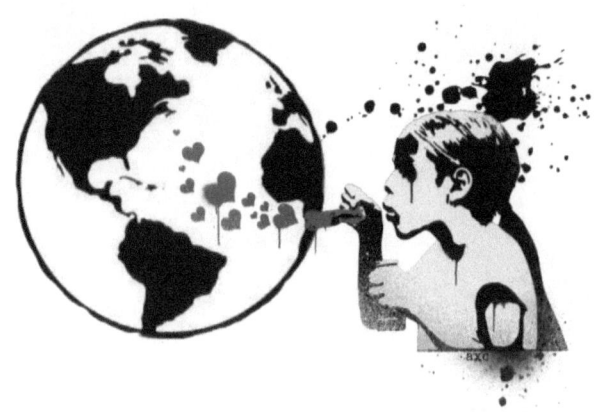

I didn't know happiness until I couldn't shake being sad. Love, until losing every bit I had. Warmth, until my bones shivered with bitter cold. Youth, until my joints cracked and ached, then I felt old. We grow a little wiser, after going through pain. We appreciate the sun a little more, after being stuck out in the rain. That's the way life goes and we don't miss most things until they're gone. Yes, that's the way it always works, perhaps joy wouldn't exist at all if not for hurt.

We were bold, we were brave, we walked into the place and took it over. We had fire in our eyes and lust in our blood, at least that's the mask that we wore. We were hiding the fear down in our bellies, the lonely down in our bones, so many miles and miles from home. We stood with men that we called brother, shipmate, yet we were still so alone.

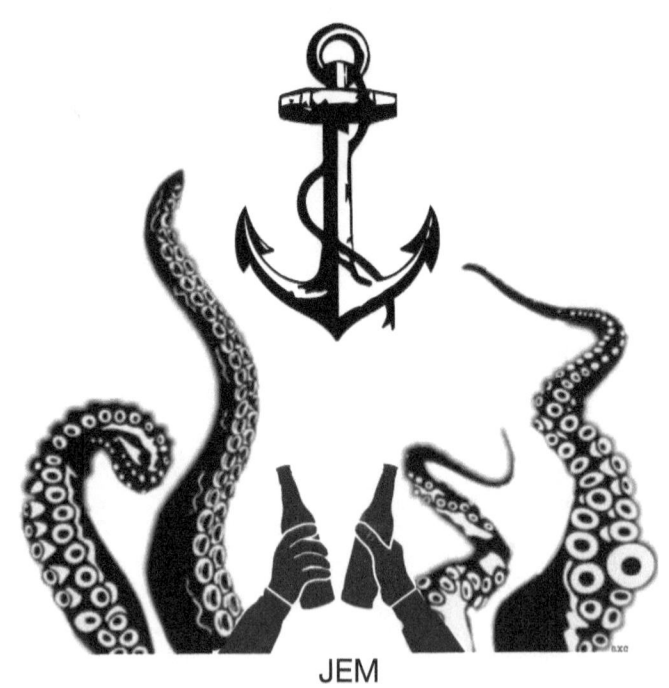

How often do we use the phrase "Don't judge me", yet we turn around and judge others by those same social standards that we protest. Can we even stand in front of the mirror without judging ourselves? It's not something I can attest, but I'm trying and doing my best to appreciate the good and learn from the rest.

I see them everywhere, the hollow ones.
They do nothing but consume, from the
moment of their birth until they're laid
down in their tomb. They're not as hard
to spot anymore. It'll be painted all
over their face, when they show you to the
door. They enjoy seeing you smile, while
they're sucking you dry. When you're
drained with nothing left, they won't
stick around to watch you cry.

I can feel you getting closer. Your
energy, it's sending signals to mine with
pings like sonar. Lost in all of the
chaos of this world since birth. Every
moment of love, happiness, misfortune, or
heartbreak keeps on bringing us closer
together. We've had to experience all of
these places and people where our current
doesn't flow, so that when we finally
meet; the connection will never break,
we'll latch on eternally. I know you're
getting closer, I feel you waking me in
the night. Your signal is getting
stronger. I've seen you in my dreams, I
felt you in my bones. I know it in my
heart, we're almost home.

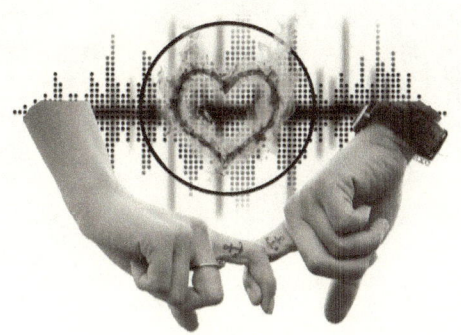

I'd often dreamed of living forever

So I thought that if I became poetry

Then my words would be around

To be found and read

And taken in through

The hearts pumping with

Passion for something more

Something greater

Something infinite

So will you for a moment

Take my hand

Let us time travel

We always wish on the shooting stars, but wouldn't it be amazing if the star you wished on wasn't shooting, fleeting, falling, dying in the blink of an eye? Wouldn't it be so surreal if the one you wished on stayed there burning for only you forever?

There's a certain pain that you never quite let go of. You don't ever share it. It's yours and yours alone to carry. Then it gets lighter, it's not so big that it fills your chest up anymore. You almost forget about it, but it's right there in your back pocket. You're afraid to let yourself be truly happy because you're scared it won't last. You're scared to let that hollow space fill up in your chest because that little reminder you keep tucked away, but as much as the little reminder protects you from further pain, it also keeps you from further love. You have to let it go if you're ever going to find the real thing.

Just for a moment

Our lips strummed the strings.

Our bodies hummed the chords

We played in harmony

A sweet melody of love echoed

Ecstasy through our bones

What have I learned. I've learned that most of all the people that really love you are the ones that have seen you make mistakes and get angry. They've seen how you can break down, but they've also seen your will to press on in the midst of your failures. They're the ones that know when you are silent. They're the ones that see you are bigger than your faults. They've been sent here to guide you. They've been here along. They'll even be here when they're gone. Love is everlasting, it changes form from one hand to another. From a goodbye to a hello. The faces may change, but the love remains intact, in time it will always replay the same. This experience was made for you. And don't you ever doubt that you're going to make it. You already have.

Let me tell you about the time that I saw God... he was standing in the mirror right in front of me and the devil, well he wasn't far behind. He was leaning over my shoulder, whispering in my ear, filling me full of doubt, filling me full of fear, but God smiled back at me because he knew it wasn't true. He gave me a long hard stare and then I knew just what to do.

You better tell them, show them, embrace them and love them something fierce or else you'll only be cheating yourself.

Don't try to make sense of it all, just believe that one day it'll all make sense and enjoy what's in front of you right now. That's called faith.

"Lost boy"

Stuck in my head, thoughts forever racing. Sometimes I'd rather be dead, than to live through what I'm facing. When did this happen, what set me off? Looking back, I've always felt kinda lost. Could it've been as a child, parents always fussing? No love in that house, only tears and cussing. Mom always depressed and down, when he came home she'd be pushed around. Hiding in my room, trying to drown it all out. Under the bed crying, as they scream and shout. Nah, I won't blame it on them, That's a coward's way out. So what then could it really be, is there even hope for someone like me? Growing up anything I tried, seemed destined to fail, with no one to help me, as my ship set sail. Somewhere along the journey, my train got derailed. Self medication had me, waking up in jail. They said be careful, when you choose your friends. Some happy beginnings, have tragic ends. Failed goals and people, such a heavy cost. Could it be, that I'm forever lost? The answer perhaps, I'll never know, but in order to change we have to grow.

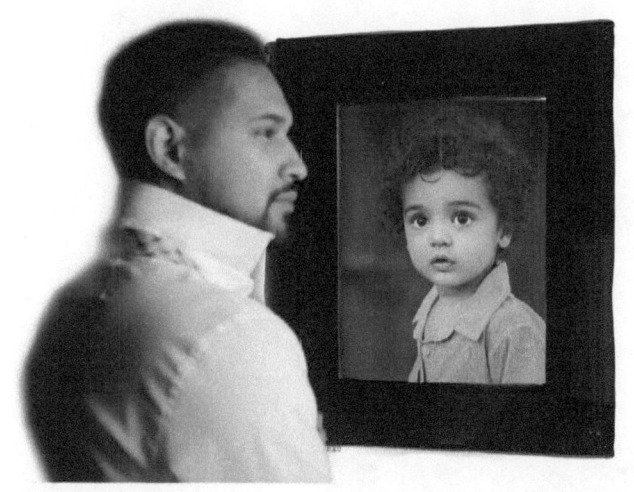

Sometimes it's hard when you're looking for someone to relate to, someone to make you feel you're not alone. Then you bump into someone unexpectedly and they make you feel at home.

If tomorrow I'd wake up and have everything I've ever lost, I wouldn't want it anyway. I'm a different person now.

Thank you so much for reading and I wish you peace, love, and light on your journey. Until the next time...

"Walk gently and love fiercely."

Acknowledgements

I'd like to acknowledge Amanda Coleman @amanda.x.coleman @a.x.c_designs for her support and skills with graphic design for illustration. I'd also like to acknowledge some of the insta-poets that have been dear friends and inspiration along the way during the last couple years. @mandymadewords @dortomysoul @tinanicholeking @m.mc.kinley @vintage_cass_marie @the.saint.atlas @eleven.twenty.four

Thank you!

www.ingramcontent.com/pod-product-compliance
Lightning Source LLC
Chambersburg PA
CBHW030647220526
45463CB00005B/1665